Modern Cla

Roll of Thunder, Hear My Cry

Mary Green

Folens Publishers

Acknowledgements

Folens allows photocopying of pages marked 'copiable page' for educational use, providing that this use is within the confines of the purchasing institution. Copiable pages should not be declared in any return in respect of any photocopying licence.

Editor: Hayley Willer
Illustrations: Martin Salisbury
Cover design: Ed Gallagher

Layout artist: Louise Pellowe
Cover image: *Three Negro Boys*, Jean Antoine Watteau (Oracle Pictures)

© 1999 Folens Limited, on behalf of the author.
Every effort has been made to contact copyright holders of material used in this book. If any have been overlooked, we will be pleased to make any necessary arrangements.

From *Roll of Thunder, Hear My Cry* by Mildred D Taylor. Copyright © 1976 by Mildred D Taylor. Used by permission of Dial Books for Young Readers, a division of Penguin Putnam Inc.

Page 34: From *To Kill a Mockingbird* by Harper Lee. Extract reproduced by permission of the publishers, Heinemann.

First published 1999 by Folens Limited, Dunstable and Dublin.
Folens Limited, Albert House, Apex Business Centre, Boscombe Road, Dunstable, LU5 4RL, United Kingdom.

ISBN 1 86202 648–3

Printed in Singapore by Craft Print.

Contents

Teachers' notes

Where textual page numbers are given, they refer to the
Puffin Books publication of *Roll of Thunder, Hear My Cry* (1976).

Background

Summary of events, Timeline (Pages 6–7)
Both sheets can be retained by students. The timeline should be used to record key events and other structural and symbolic features. Regular referral will help students remember details.

Background to the novel (Page 8)
The historic and cultural factors that influence the book are given here along with biographical details of the author and a note on the narrative voice. Some references to relevant scenes and characters in the novel are also given.

The characters

Who's who? – major characters,
Who's who? – minor characters (Pages 9–10)
These two activity sheets cover the major characters and some minor ones. They should be retained by students for reference. The minor characters have been included because of their relation to the main themes: racism, segregation, violence and non-violence, family and community.

Cassie, Mama (Mary Logan), Papa (David Logan), Stacey, T J Avery, Uncle Hammer, Big Ma (Pages 11–17)
These sheets cover the main characters, and once completed can be used for easy referral.
Students should be discouraged from writing at length. Notes and quick references are more appropriate.

Who says? (Page 18)
There are many important quotations in the book. This exercise asks students to identify who is speaking, to whom, what is being discussed and where the quotations appear in the book. Please note that a similar quotation to Question 3 is spoken by Papa to Cassie on Page 143, Chapter 8.

Different perspectives (Page 19)
Students should be reminded, when undertaking Question 5, that the monologue at the top of the sheet is not actually spoken by Uncle Hammer. There may be some aspects students do not agree with. For example, how conscious is Uncle Hammer of the consequences of his own temper?

Final chapters – 11 and 12

Roll of thunder (Page 20)
The inclusion of the blues song here could be seen as a symbol of both the punishment inflicted on T J and his family by the Wallaces and the Simms, and the determination of David Logan to take courageous action. It is also a precursor to the climax of the novel.

T J's story (Page 21)
Students are asked to summarise the main points of T J's account of the robbery. The prompts provide assistance.

The children's action (Page 22)
The main task here requires students to consider what series of events might have occurred if Cassie's wishes had been followed. Various possibilities should occur to students, but the essential issue is not the probable events but an understanding of the way in which character can affect plot.

At the Averys' (Page 23)
Students are asked to recall the events at the end of Chapter 11 in which T J is blamed for the Barnett robbery. It is a comparatively simple exercise. A more difficult question follows that requires an understanding of T J's character and circumstances.

Waiting (Page 24)
Students are asked to consider the significance of the paragraph that appears just before the climax to the novel and to rewrite it from an adult's perspective, rather than from a child's.

The burning fields (Page 25)
All the quotations relate to the circumstances of the fire. Students need to understand not only that David Logan began it deliberately, but how and why. The fire can be seen as briefly uniting the black and white communities in their attempt to control it.

Language and style

Speech and dialect (Page 26)
Students are asked to decipher dialect and to identify techniques used by the author to make speech seem authentic.

Similes and metaphors (Page 27)
Simile and metaphor can sometimes be confused and this sheet is useful for those students who experience difficulty in remembering which is which.

Images (Page 28)
This sheet is more difficult than the previous one and is suitable for those students who have some understanding of simile and metaphor.

Symbol (Page 29)
There are several symbols and motifs running through the book, many of them nature symbols. The significance of the seasons and the weather in marking events could be discussed with students.

Teachers' notes

The narrative voice (Page 30)
It can be difficult for students to appreciate the quality of the narrative voice. The 'Author's Note' allows a comparison to be made between the narrative voice and the voice of the novel. The two passages on this sheet, though similar in content, have marked differences.

The night men (Pages 31–32)
Students should tackle these sheets after completing work on the use of language in the novel. Please note Mr Morrison's 'Old Testament' language and the depiction of the night men as 'devilish' with connotations of the Four Horsemen of the Apocalypse.

Screen adaptation (Page 33)
This sheet can be used by those English departments that hold the BBC adaptation of the novel. Students are asked to focus on two scenes in order to consider what is lost and gained and which scene adapts more easily. The teacher may wish to discuss the greater visual impact and dramatic tension of the second scene (the cotton fields on fire). He or she may wish to discuss the visual impact and dramatic tension of the fire as particularly suitable for adaptation to film.

Making comparisons (Page 34)
A passage from *Roll of Thunder, Hear My Cry* is compared with *To Kill a Mockingbird* by Harper Lee, encouraging students to draw on other literature when studying texts. Though the two books share obvious similarities, there are also differences. In particular, the former is written from the black perspective and takes a less hopeful view than the latter.

Themes

Racism (Page 35)
Students are asked to discuss the different kinds of racism found in the book. Stacey's treatment of Jeremy is based on the consequences for him of mixing with a white boy but also on his personal feelings of unease. Students may wish to discuss whether or not this is an inevitable consequence of segregation and inequality.

Segregation (Page 36)
The teacher may wish to discuss the ways in which segregation is manifested in the novel before students begin the tasks. The examples may fit more than one category but the answers given on Page 48 identify the main ones.

Violence (Page 37)
The sequence of events here depict Cassie's humiliation at the hands of Lillian Jean and Mr Simms in Chapter 5. Students should identify the events and place the illustrations in order.

Family life (Page 38)
Students are asked to identify a number of families in *Roll of Thunder, Hear My Cry*, and appreciate the importance of family life in the novel.

The land (Page 39)
Students are asked to consider what the land means to various characters in the novel and to write about it from Mr Jamison's perspective. They should refer to Chapter 7 to gain a fuller picture of his personality and attitudes. The teacher may wish to discuss David Logan's burning of the cotton fields in Chapter 12 and Mr Jamison's response to this. The land can also be seen as a motif and teachers may wish to discuss this when using '**Symbols**' (Page 29).

Essay practice

Quotations as evidence (Page 40)
Students are presented with different ways to use quotations effectively and are given tasks based around using quotations in different ways.

Stacey and Jeremy (Page 41)
Help is given to contrast two characters. Teachers may need to discuss the way in which Stacey and Jeremy are divided by race, and why David Logan discourages the friendship between them.

Family influences (Page 42)
Students are guided through a common and straightforward essay question.

Black history (Page 43)
This sheet gives advice to those students likely to take a higher-level paper. It involves writing an essay on the historical background to the novel.

Exam practice

Exam passage (Page 44)
A selected passage is taken from the novel and a series of questions follow.

Exam questions (Page 45)
These questions are suitable for students taking a foundation paper.

Further exam questions (Page 46)
These more challenging questions are suitable for students taking a higher-level paper.

Answers

Selected answers (Pages 47–48)
This page provides answers relating to some of the questions that appear on the activity sheets.

Summary of events

FOCUS

- To revise the main events of *Roll of Thunder, Hear My Cry*.

Introduction

The novel covers many events over 12 months, from the beginning of the school year in Chapter 1 to late summer in Chapter 12. The main themes of racism, violence, family life and the land run through the book.

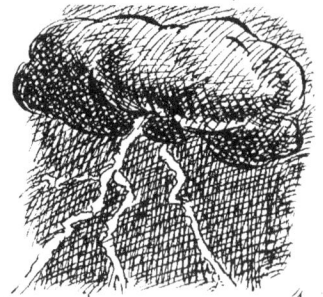

- **Chapters 1–4**
  - The Logan children walk to school with T J Avery and his brother. They talk of racist burnings in the area. The bus carrying white pupils to school covers the children in dirt. Little Man's rejection of the books at school sparks an incident.
  - Mr Morrison is to stay with the Logans to protect them in Papa's absence. A racist attack on the Berrys results in no action being taken despite the Wallaces' guilt.
  - Heavy rain results in the Logan children being drenched by the school bus. In revenge, the children dig a ditch in which the bus becomes trapped. They fear retaliation from racist attackers, 'the night men'.
  - Stacey is blamed for T J's dishonesty and follows him to the Wallaces' store (where the black community is obliged to shop but which is boycotted by the Logans). Mr Morrison intervenes. Big Ma tells Cassie about the Logan heritage.
  - The children are taken to see Mr Berry who has been badly burned by the Wallaces.

- **Chapters 5–8**
  - Cassie experiences discrimination at the hands of Lillian Jean Simms.
  - Uncle Hammer arrives for Christmas and Cassie tells him how mortified she feels. He wants to retaliate but is prevented. Mama teaches Cassie the complexities of racism.
  - Stacey is given a new coat by Uncle Hammer. T J is jealous and humiliates Stacey who disowns the coat (subsequently giving it to T J).
  - The Wallaces mistake Uncle Hammer's Packard for Harlan Granger's, a white landowner, and show their respect. Mama fears the consequences.
  - Christmas approaches. Papa returns. Mr Morrison recounts his memories. Jeremy Simms brings a present for Stacey who accepts it awkwardly.
  - Mr Jamison, a white lawyer and friend of the Logans, sets out documents to secure the Logans' land for them. Harlan Granger objects both to this and to the boycott of the Wallace store.
  - Seeking revenge on Lillian Jean, Cassie resorts to deception and violence.
  - Mary Logan loses her post as teacher, partly as a result of T J's slanders. He is rejected by the Logan children.

- **Chapters 9–12**
  - It is Spring, the end of the school year. T J has forged a disastrous friendship with the older Simms boys. The boycott of the Wallace store begins to fail. Papa is attacked and injured but saved by Mr Morrison. The family struggle financially. Further racist incidents occur.
  - The bank, influenced by Harlan Granger, demands that the Logans' mortgage be paid. Uncle Hammer provides the money.
  - T J is involved in robbing the Barnetts' store with the Simms brothers. Although innocent of injuring the Barnetts he is blamed. T J seeks help from Stacey. A lynch mob arrives at T J's house. Mr Jamison holds them back and, at great risk, Papa sets alight the cotton fields as a decoy. T J is taken into custody and we learn that Mr Barnett has died. The novel ends with the probability that T J will be executed or sent to the chain gang.

MODERN CLASSICS: *Roll of Thunder, Hear My Cry*   © Folens (copiable page)

Timeline

FOCUS

- To make a timeline that shows, at a glance, where the key events occur, helping you to recall information.

- Use the '**Summary of events**' sheet to mark key points on the line below, particularly those that are related to the main themes. Remember that the duration of the novel is one year and change is often marked by seasonal events, the weather and the effect this has on the land. Include chapter and page references.

Background to the novel

FOCUS

- To understand the economic and social conditions in which *Roll of Thunder, Hear My Cry* is set.

- Read the information below carefully and retain this sheet for your own reference.

Slavery and segregation

After the American Civil War in which the North won, the South could only be readmitted to the Union if slavery was abolished. There was great resentment in the South. Southern plantation owners continued to use black people to work the land in much the same way as they always had. After slavery was abolished, Reconstruction, which was a failed attempt to move closer to equality, was followed by a backlash. The Southern States reintroduced racist laws and the segregation of the black and white communities remained. This is particularly evident in the novel's depiction of the well-equipped Jefferson Davis County School for white students and the ill-equipped Great Faith Elementary School for black students.

Race

Racism, symbolised by 'the night men', is at the heart of the novel. White supremacist groups, such as the Ku Klux Klan, were very active in Mississippi during the 1930s, the time at which the story is set. Lynchings, burnings and other violent acts were common and the law did little to protect the black community or bring the perpetrators to justice. The sense of fear and anxiety felt by the Logan children, the stories told around the hearth and the consequences for T J dominate the novel. There is no resolution in the final chapters and the outlook is largely pessimistic. While we are left with the sense that the Logan family will survive all hardships we do not feel that racism will eventually be overcome or even diminish.

The Depression

The 1930s was a time of severe economic depression. Poverty and unemployment were high in both the South and the North and these economic conditions and social evils helped to fuel racism. In the South the cotton plantations were affected and people often had to seek work elsewhere. (David Logan, for example, manages to hold down insecure work on the railroad, Chapter 1.)

Mildred D Taylor

The author, an African American born in Jackson, Mississippi, and brought up in Ohio, refers in the preface of her book to her father as a 'master storyteller' who kept black history alive. She would have been well aware of the conditions in the Southern States during the 1930s, and as a student at Toledo University during the 1960s, she would have been aware of the Civil Rights Movement, when such leaders as Martin Luther King and Malcolm X were influential. After studying at university she worked in Ethiopia and at the University of Colorado, helping to construct a black-studies programme.

The narrator

The narrator is Cassie Logan, the second child of the Logan family, and the events in the novel are seen through her eyes.

Who's who? – major characters

FOCUS

- To revise the characteristics of a number of major characters.

- Read this sheet carefully. Use it as a reference to the major characters in *Roll of Thunder, Hear My Cry*.

Mary Logan (Mama)
Mother, teacher. Strong moral sense, courageous, hates injustice.

Cassie Logan
Main character; an able, assertive nine-year-old girl. Fiery temper, loyal. Narrator of the story.

David Logan (Papa)
Father. Owns land, railroad worker. Caring, courageous.

Stacey Logan
Cassie's twelve-year-old brother. Trustworthy, loyal, supports his brothers and sister.

Caroline Logan (Big Ma)
Papa's mother. Strong, archetypal figure, storyteller. Knowledge of herbal medicines. Reminds children of their heritage.

Uncle Hammer
Papa's brother. Has moved north. Tough-minded, stylish, successful, fiery temper.

T J Avery
Stacey's older friend. Poor, easily led. Becomes the victim of extreme racism.

Who's who? – minor characters

● Read this sheet carefully. Use it as a reference to the minor characters in *Roll of Thunder, Hear My Cry*.

Christopher-John Logan
Cassie's brother, 'a short round boy of seven', friendly, passive, well-meaning. He becomes more assertive as the story develops.

Little Man (Clayton Chester Logan)
At six years old, he is the youngest in the family. Clean and meticulous. He is confident, and will speak out against unjust treatment.

Mr Jamison
A white lawyer whose sympathies lie with the black community. He supports the Logans, but he knows they cannot win. Shows bravery when saving T J from the lynch mob.

Mr Granger
White racist, whose beliefs are rooted in the past. Powerful landowner, pitted against the Logans.

Mr Morrison
Takes care of the Logans when Papa is away, 'a human tree in height' and although middle-aged, still a man of great strength.

Jeremy Simms
A friend of the Logans who is at odds with his family and the white community. Able and sensitive, he represents, like Mr Jamison, a positive force in the book.

R W Simms and Melvin Simms
Racist older brothers of Jeremy Simms and Lillian Jean Simms. Instrumental in T J's downfall.

Cassie

● To explore Cassie's character.

● Make notes about Cassie under the headings below, and use them to help you write assignments and essays. Include quotations together with page numbers to support what you say.

Age, appearance, position in the family

How she regards others and the world around her

Character traits: strengths and weaknesses

What others think about her

How others regard her

How she matures during the novel: what she learns from events and characters

Mama (Mary Logan)

FOCUS

● To explore Mama's character.

● Make notes about Mama under the headings below, and use them to help you write assignments and essays. Include quotations together with page numbers to support what you say.

Age, appearance, profession, position in the family, status in the black community

Important actions taken, which are lessons for her children

Character traits: strengths and weaknesses

What she learns or what is reinforced by the end of the novel

How others regard her: how this varies inside and outside the family

Papa (David Logan)

FOCUS

- To explore Papa's character.

- Make notes about Papa under the headings below, and use them to help you write assignments and essays. Include quotations together with page numbers to support what you say.

Age, appearance, employment, position in the family, status in the black community

Important actions taken, which are lessons for his children

Character traits: strengths and weaknesses (contrast with Mama)

What he learns or what is reinforced by the end of the novel

How others regard him

Stacey

FOCUS

- To explore Stacey's character.

- Make notes about Stacey under the headings below, and use them to help you write assignments and essays. Include quotations together with page numbers to support what you say.

Age, appearance, position in the family

How he regards others and the world around him

Character traits: strengths and weaknesses (contrast with Cassie)

What he learns or what is reinforced by the end of the novel

How others regard him

T J Avery

- To explore T J Avery's character.

- Make notes about T J Avery under the headings below, and use them to help you write assignments and essays. Include quotations together with page numbers to support what you say.

Age, appearance, family situation

Important incidents in which he is included

Character traits: strengths and weaknesses (contrast with Stacey)

His situation by the end of the novel: is it inevitable?

How others regard him (contrast Cassie's attitude to him with Stacey's)

Uncle Hammer

FOCUS

- To explore Uncle Hammer's character.

- Make notes about Uncle Hammer under the headings below, and use them to help you write assignments and essays. Include quotations together with page numbers to support what you say.

Age, appearance, position in the family

How he regards others

Character traits: strengths and weaknesses, similarities and dissimilarities to others in the family

How events reinforce his views

How he is regarded by the black and white communities and what he represents in the novel

Big Ma

FOCUS

● To explore Big Ma's character.

● Make notes about Big Ma under the headings below, and use them to help you write assignments and essays. Include quotations together with page numbers to support what you say.

Age, appearance, position in the family, status in the black community

How she regards others

Character traits: strengths and weaknesses

How her action at the end of the novel confirms her character

How others, particularly the children, regard her

Who says?

- In the spaces provided, write down who is speaking, to whom, what is being discussed and on which page the quotation appears.

Said by _____

To _____

About _____

Page _____

1. "It will be easy enough for anyone to see whose responsibility it is ... by opening any seventh-grade book. Because tomorrow I'm going to 'mess them up' too."

Said by _____

To _____

About _____

_____

Page _____

2. "All that belongs to you. You ain't never had to live on nobody's place but your own ..."

3. "What we do have is some choice over what we make of our lives once we're here."

Said by _____

To _____

About _____

_____

Page _____

Said by _____

To _____

About _____

_____

Page _____

4. "I ain't never lied to y'all, y'all know that ... Well, I ... I wish I could lie to y'all now."

5. "I'm a Southerner, born and bred, but that doesn't mean I approve of all that goes on here, and there are a lot of other white people who feel the same ... (but) ... there aren't enough of those same white people who would admit how they feel ..."

Said by _____

To _____

About _____

_____

Page _____

Said by _____

To _____

About _____

_____

Page _____

6. "It gets hot like this and folks get dissatisfied with life, they start looking 'round for somebody to take it out on ... I don't want it to be you."

MODERN CLASSICS: *Roll of Thunder, Hear My Cry* © Folens (copiable page)

Different perspectives

- To consider Uncle Hammer's character traits and write two monologues from the perspectives of two characters.

1. Read the following imagined monologue by Uncle Hammer, about his view of life.

> I always had a taste for style and a man can barely keep his dignity in Mississippi, never mind clothe himself. Besides, my temper's got the devil in it and sooner or later ... well you can guess. So I makes for Chicago. Maybe it ain't perfect but I was right impressed by that city. A man can earn a man's wage. And I was determined to make good. But, I worry about the family and though I feel some bitterness – with the German war an' all, an' the way they still treat us – I like to come back home, to our land.

2. Underline the points in the monologue that tell you what Uncle Hammer's main character traits are.

3. Choose two characters from below and list their main character traits. (Refer to any notes and references you may have made on other sheets.)

  – Cassie
  – Little Man
  – Jeremy Simms
  – Mr Morrison
  – Christopher-John

4. Write a monologue of 100 words for each of your two characters. Try to capture the character's dialect, if you can. Think of the characters as though they are talking to the reader.

5. A character's attitudes often affect what happens to them in the novel, just as what happens to them can affect their attitudes. Write 100 words explaining what aspects of Uncle Hammer's character might have made him decide to leave Mississippi and go north.

6. Now write 100 words saying what events brought Uncle Hammer back in Chapter 10 and what this tells you about his character.

Roll of thunder

FOCUS

- To understand the lines of the blues song that gives the book its title.

1. Read the following lines of the blues song included at the beginning of Chapter 11.

Roll of thunder
   hear my cry
Over the water
   bye and bye
Ole man comin'
   down the line
Whip in hand to
   beat me down
But I *ain't*
   gonna let him
Turn me 'round

2. Explain what the lines above mean and where you think they are set. There are clues in the third and sixth lines.

3. What is the mood of the lines? Consider these possibilities and then explain why you chose the words that you did.

long-suffering   defiant   hopeful   defeated

hopeless   angry   pleading

feeble   calm

4. Why do you think the author has chosen to include the lines of the song at the beginning of Chapter 11?

5. In what way are the lines also relevant to Chapter 12?

T J's story

- To understand T J's account of what happens in the Barnetts' mercantile to compare with events later in the Chapter.

- Using the following prompts, summarise the main events described by T J in Chapter 11.

I. **T J, R W and Melvin go straight to Strawberry after leaving Great Faith Church ...**

_____

_____

_____

2. **T J slips through a small window ...**

_____

_____

_____

3. **As Melvin reaches for the box, Mr Barnett appears ...**

_____

_____

_____

_____

4. **Once outside, T J wants to go home ...**

_____

_____

_____

5. **After approximately an hour in the truck ...**

_____

_____

_____

The children's action

FOCUS

- To consider what events might have occurred if Cassie's wishes had been followed.

Introduction

Cassie's view of what should be done about T J in Chapter 11 differs from Stacey's. This displays their different personalities, and the choice they make affects the storyline.

1. Read the following extract from Chapter 11.

> "Stacey?" I whispered, afraid of what he might do.
> As far back as I could remember, Stacey had felt a
> responsibility for T J. I had never really understood
> why. Perhaps he felt that even a person as despicable
> as T J needed someone he could call 'friend', or perhaps
> he sensed T J's vulnerability better than T J did
> himself. "Stacey, you ain't going, are you?"

2. a. What does Cassie threaten to do immediately after this passage?

   b. What does she actually do?

   c. What is the outcome of the children's action?

3. Do you think it would have been better to do what Cassie wanted? Consider what difference it might have made to the following and write your answer in 200 words.

   a. T J, David Logan, Christopher-John and Little Man.

   b. A satisfactory storyline.

MODERN CLASSICS: *Roll of Thunder, Hear My Cry* © Folens (copiable page)

At the Averys'

FOCUS

- To become aware of T J's account of the robbery and what happens to him afterwards.

1. Write a paragraph explaining what is happening in the following pictures.

2. Write a second paragraph comparing T J's personality with R W Simms' and Melvin Simms'. Say why you think T J is easy to manipulate.

Waiting

FOCUS

● To consider the significance of the paragraph that appears just before the climax of the novel.

Introduction

There is a period of tension in Chapter 12 between the departure of David Logan and the beginning of the fire, in which the family waits in silence. This is part of the structure of the last two chapters. It can be seen as the 'calm before the storm', reminding us of the symbolism of the book.

1. Read the following extract from the novel.

Mama pushed us back into her room, where Big Ma fell upon her knees and prayed a powerful prayer. Afterward both Mama and Big Ma changed their clothes, then we sat, very quiet, as the heat crept sticky and wet through our clothing and the thunder banged menacingly overhead. Mama, her knuckles tight against her skin as she gripped the arms of the chair, looked down upon Christopher-John, Little Man, and me, our eyes wide awake with fear. 'I don't suppose it would do any good to put you to bed,' she said quietly. We looked up at her. She did not mean to have an answer; we gave none, and nothing else was said as the night minutes crept past and the waiting pressed as heavily upon us as the heat.

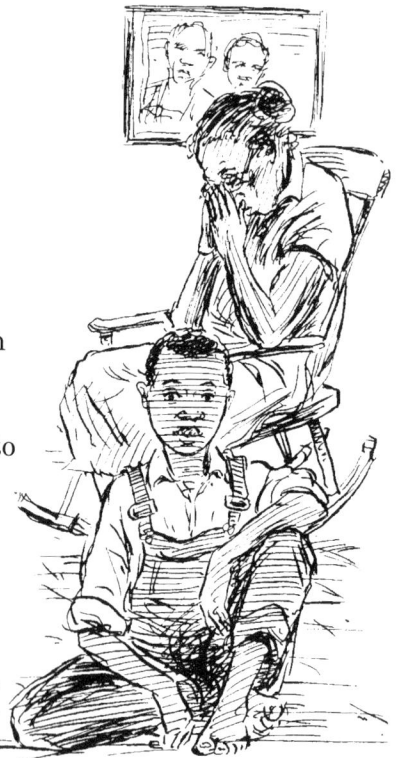

2. Underline all the phrases and clauses in the above extract that indicate tension, fear and heat.

3. Write the description again, but from Big Ma's point of view, rather than Cassie's. Use suitable images and similes. Remember that Big Ma has considerable experience and wisdom compared to Cassie.

4. Imagine the scene in your mind and write three sentences summing up the different ways in which the following characters respond to the situation: Big Ma, Mama, the children.

MODERN CLASSICS: *Roll of Thunder, Hear My Cry*   © Folens (copiable page)

The burning fields

FOCUS

- To understand that the fire is significant in more than one way.

1. The following comments are made in Chapter 12. Decide who is speaking, to whom, and what is being discussed.

a.

"Funny thing. That fire come up from that lightning and struck one of them wooden fence posts, I reckon, and sparked that cotton."

Said by _____

To _____

About _____

b.

"... and Mr Morrison come and got me and then them men come down here to fight the fire and didn't nobody have to fight nobody."

Said by _____

To _____

About _____

c.

"It's better, I think, that you stay clear of this whole thing now, ... and don't give anybody cause to think about you at all ..."

Said by _____

To _____

About _____

2. a. Discuss with a partner in what way the fire is a unifying force as well as a destructive one. Also talk about why fire, in particular, is so significant. (Think about the night men, references to the Bible, etc.) Make notes.

2. b. Develop your notes into an answer of 300 words addressing the three issues in 2.a.

MODERN CLASSICS: *Roll of Thunder, Hear My Cry*

Speech and dialect

FOCUS

- To decipher dialect and to identify techniques used by the author to make speech seem authentic.

Introduction

There is more than one way of speaking in *Roll of Thunder, Hear My Cry* but the most common is the local dialect.

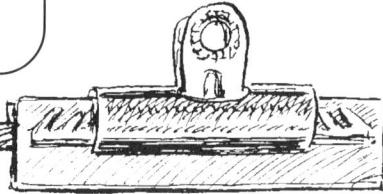

1. Write down what these expressions mean and check any that you are not sure of.

   a. 'cuttin' up'

   b. 'bootlegging'

   c. 'running his mouth off'

   d. 'mopin' 'round'

   e. 'Yankee carpetbaggers'

   f. 'a sorrowful long time'

   g. 'gets title to a place'

   h. 'traveling store'

2. Write out the following in standard English. Decide who is speaking and where in the book the passage appears.

   > "Sho' was. He was carpenterin' up there and my papa took me in with him to Vicksburg – we was tenant farmin' 'bout thirty miles from there – to see 'bout gettin' a store-bought rocker for my mama, and there was ole Paul Edward workin' in that furniture shop just as big. Had himself a good job, but that 'ole job wasn't what he wanted. He wanted himself some land. Kept on and kept on talkin' 'bout land, and then this place come up for sell."

3. What techniques does the author use to encourage us to read the words as they would have been spoken?

4. In what way does the following speech differ from the speech above? Again, say who is speaking and at what point in the story. Say why you think this character speaks differently.

   > "White people may demand our respect, but what we give them is not respect but fear. What we give to our own people is far more important because it's given freely. Now you may have to call Lillian Jean 'Miss' because the white people say so, but you'll also call our own young ladies at church 'Miss' because you really do respect them."

MODERN CLASSICS: *Roll of Thunder, Hear My Cry* © Folens (copiable page)

Similes and metaphors

FOCUS

• To understand simile and metaphor.

Introduction
Writers use a range of techniques to express their ideas. Simile, in particular, is common but metaphor is also used in passages in the novel where the writer wants to create a particular effect or mood.

You are going to distinguish between similes and metaphors.
To help you, remember the following.

– A simile will compare one thing with another
'*He had himself a mind like a steel trap.*'

– A metaphor will describe one thing in terms of another
'*The charred skeletons of broken stalks.*'

• First underline the simile or metaphor in the examples below.
Then find the reference to each one in the book and explain:

– what it tells us about the person or thing that is described
– what sense or senses it appeals to
– who or what it refers to and why.

1. 'He would stay there for a while, walking on cat's feet through the quiet yard ...'
(Chapter 11)

2. 'Before us the narrow, sun-splotched road wound like a lazy red serpent ...' (Chapter 1)

3. '... she was combing her hair, which fanned her head like an enormous black halo.'
(Chapter 6)

4. 'The man was a human tree in height, towering high above Papa's six feet two inches.' (Chapter 2)

5. '... a bus bore down on him spewing clouds of red dust like a huge yellow dragon breathing fire.' (Chapter 1)

6. 'She always smelled of sunshine and soap.'
(Chapter 6)

Images

Introduction

Imagery is a term that is used to cover simile and metaphor as well as other expressions of ideas and feelings. However, images are slightly different from similes and metaphors. All three appeal to a range of senses, but an image is fundamental to expressive writing and describes the object rather than comparing or replacing it. However, an image can also suggest something else behind the words.

1. In pairs, say what sense or senses the following images appeal to and describe the mood each one evokes. Then, on your own, find the images in the book and explain the contexts in which they occur.

a. 'Mr Morrison sat singing soft and low into the long night, chanting to the approaching thunder.' (Page 194, Chapter 11)

b. '... the dust swelled up in rolls of billowing clouds behind us.' (Page 114, Chapter 6)

c. '... a choice sugar-cured ham brought from the smokehouse awaited its turn in the oven.' (Page 120, Chapter 7)

d. '... Mama started, but Papa enfolded her slender hand in his ...' (Page 122, Chapter 7)

e. 'I was eager to be in the fields again, to feel the furrowed rows of damp, soft earth beneath my feet ...' (Page 158, Chapter 9)

f. '... the waning light of day swiftly deepened into a fine velvet night ...' (Page 120, Chapter 7)

2. Write your own images to describe the following. Use adjectives or adverbs, but avoid similes and metaphors.
   a. A small child comforting her grandmother.
   b. The tension before a fight between two people.
   c. The landscape after a shower of rain.

Symbol

FOCUS

- To understand the significance of symbols in the novel.

Introduction

A symbol is a representation of something and often occurs in prose and poetry. There are several symbols in the novel. For example, it could be said that the Packard represents wealth and power.

1. Explain what you think the following symbols represent.

The pearl-handled pistol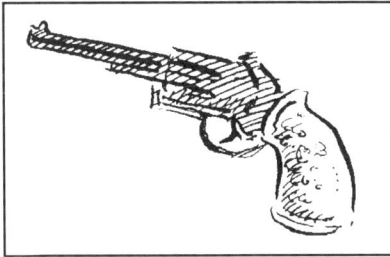

 The fig tree

The night men

 The thunder

2. The seasons and the weather can be seen as symbols. They mark the story as it unfolds over a year in the life of the black community. Say which season and what weather is linked to each of the following.

    a. The beginning of the school year. (Chapter 1)

    b. When all the Logans are gathered together to celebrate. (Chapter 7)

    c. The end of the school year. (Chapter 9)

    d. The last night of the revival. (Chapter 10)

    e. The last page of the book.

3. Explain what you think the seasons and weather could represent in a–e above and how they are associated with important events. The first has been done for you.

    a. The dusty, carefree days of Summer giving way to the rain of Autumn can be seen to represent the loss of freedom and the restriction and unhappiness that school brings. The important event at this time is 'the Jefferson Davis school bus incident', when the Logan children are splashed with mud, and are humiliated.

The narrative voice

FOCUS

- To compare the narrative voice (the thoughts and commentary on the action) with the 'voice' in the 'Author's Note' to help you to understand how narrative voices vary.

1. Read the passage below. Show how you can tell the narrative voice is a child's. Underline verbs, proper nouns and any other words or phrases you think indicate this.

Here, Cassie is looking back, considering what her father once told her about the importance of the land.

I looked at Papa strangely when he said that, for I knew that all the land did not belong to me. Some of it belonged to Stacey, Christopher-John, and Little Man, not to mention the part that belonged to Big Ma, Mama, and Uncle Hammer, Papa's older brother who lived in Chicago. But Papa never divided the land in his mind; it was simply Logan land. For it he would work the long, hot summer pounding steel; Mama would teach and run the farm; Big Ma, in her sixties, would work like a woman of twenty in the fields and keep the house; and the boys and I would wear threadbare clothing washed to dishwater color; but always, the taxes and the mortgage would be paid. Papa said that one day I would understand. I wondered.

(Chapter 1)

2. Now, read the following passage. Carry out a similar task to Question 1, but show how the narrative voice is an adult's. Compare the choice of words with the above passage and consider the content of the passage as well as the language.

Here, the author is looking back considering her father's skill as a storyteller.

... I learned a history not then written in books but one passed from generation to generation on the steps of moonlit porches and beside dying fires in one-room houses, a history of great-grandparents and of slavery and of the days following slavery; of those who lived still not free, yet who would not let their spirits be enslaved. From my father the storyteller I learned to respect the past, to respect my own heritage and myself. From my father the man I learned even more, for he was endowed with a special grace that made him tower above other men. He was warm and steadfast, a man whose principles would not bend, and he had within him a rare strength ...

(Author's Note – preface to the novel)

3. Write up your notes in two paragraphs, explaining the differences between the two narrative voices.

MODERN CLASSICS: *Roll of Thunder, Hear My Cry* © Folens (copiable page)

The night men

Introduction

Mr Morrison's memories are told in vivid language below (Pages 121–122, Chapter 7). They serve to emphasise the theme of prejudice in the novel and give us an understanding of his character. To appreciate this, it helps if you can identify and discuss the language used.

"... They come down like ghosts that Christmas of seventy-six. Them was hard times like now and my family was living in a shantytown right outside Shreveport. Reconstruction was just 'bout over then, and them Northern soldiers was tired of being in the South and they didn't hardly care 'bout no black folks in shantytown. And them Southern whites, they was tired of the Northern soldiers and free Negroes, and they was trying to turn things back 'round to how they used to be. And the colored folks ... well, we was just tired. Warn't hardly no work, and during them years I s'pose it was jus' 'bout as hard being free as it was being a slave ...

"That night they come – I can remember just as good – it was cold, so cold we had to huddle all 'gainst each other just trying to keep warm, and two boys – 'bout eighteen or nineteen, I reckon – come knocking on my daddy's door. They was scairt, clean out of their heads with fright. They'd just come back from Shreveport. Some white woman done accused them of molestin' her and they didn't know nowhere to run so they come up to my daddy's 'cause he had a good head and he was big, bigger than me. He was strong too. So strong he could break a man's leg easy as if he was snapping a twig – I seen him do it that night. And the white folks was scairt of him. But my daddy didn't hardly have time to finish hearing them boys' story when them devilish night men swept down –"

✳   ✳   ✳

"... swept down like locusts," he continued in a faraway voice. "Burst in on us with their Rebel sabers, hacking and killing, burning us out. Didn't care who they kilt. We warn't nothing to them. No better than dogs. Kilt babies and old women. Didn't matter."

He gazed into the fire.

"My sisters got kilt in they fire, but my Mama got me out ..." His voice faded and he touched the scars on his neck. "She tried to get back into the house to save the girls, but she couldn't. Them night men was all over her and she threw me – just threw me like I was a ball – hard as she could, trying to get me away from them. Then she fought. Fought like a wild thing right 'side my daddy.

✳   ✳   ✳

"But my mama and daddy they loved each other and they loved us children, and that Christmas they fought them demons out of hell like avenging angels of the Lord." He turned back toward the fire and grew very quiet; then he raised his head and looked at us. "They died that night. Them night men kilt 'em. Some folks tell me I can't remember what happened that Christmas – I warn't hardly six years old – but I remembers all right. I makes myself remember."

The night men (continued)

FOCUS

● To identify and understand the use of language in the novel.

● When answering the questions below you should annotate the passage. For example, you could identify similes in one colour, symbols in another and so on. Read through all the questions first.

1. Explain in five sentences what the passage is about. Why was it ' "as hard being free as being a slave" '?

2. a. Most of Mr Morrison's speech is in dialect. Underline three expressions he uses frequently.
   b. Explain why Mr Morrison's local dialect is appropriate for this passage.
   c. In what way does the use of dashes and ellipses add to this?

3. a. From time to time Mr Morrison uses similes. Underline six examples.
   b. Which are religious similes? Where do you think they come from? What does this tell you about Mr Morrison's background?
   c. How does the use of simile give the passage additional impact?

4. a. Who are the night men?
   b. What are the night men a symbol of? How is this linked to the main theme of the novel?
   c. Find an image in the passage that gives the night men a religious connotation and describe it.

5. Why is this passage untypical of Mr Morrison? What is he usually like and in what way does the passage give you an insight into his character?

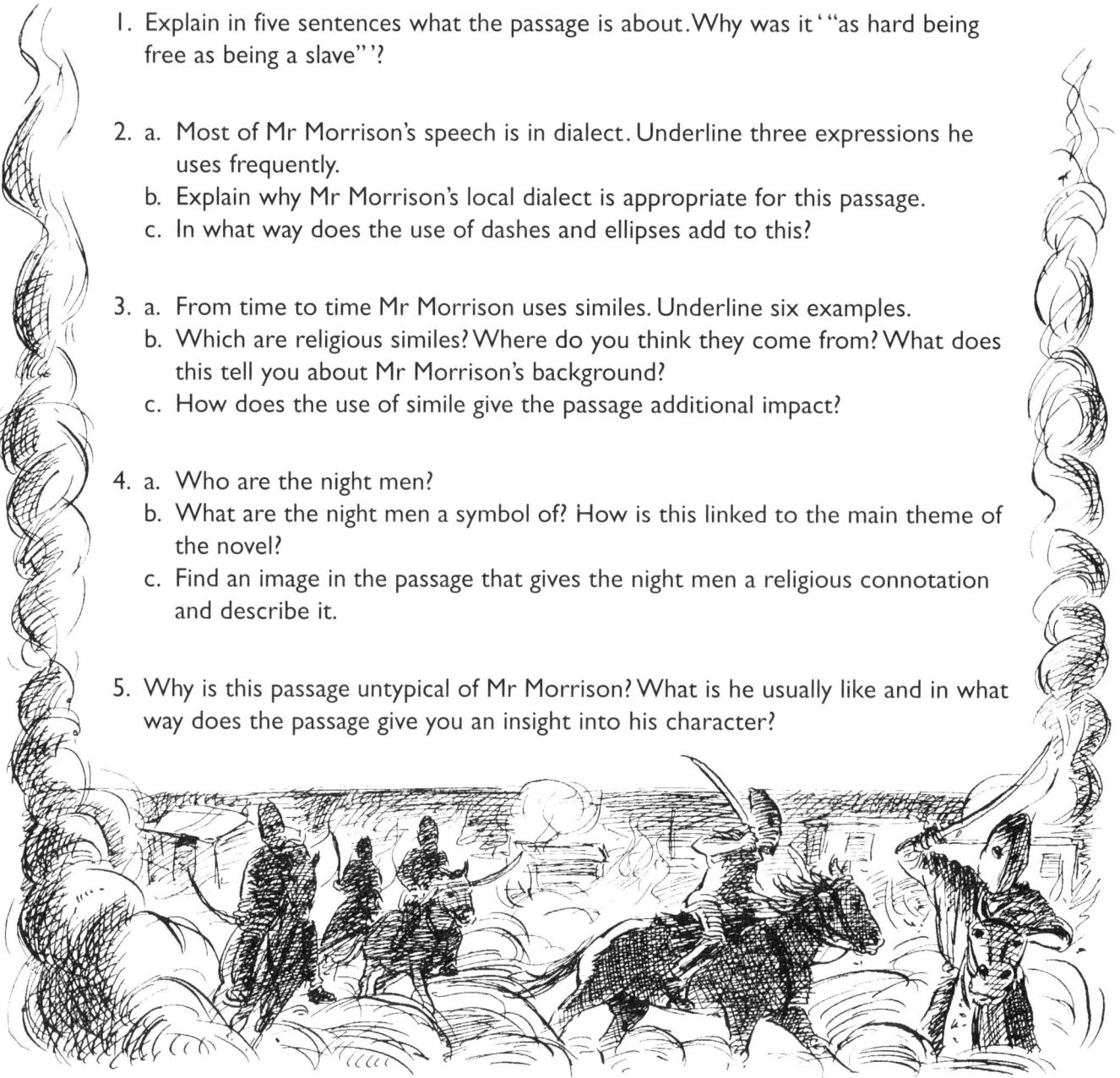

MODERN CLASSICS: *Roll of Thunder, Hear My Cry* © Folens (copiable page)

Screen adaptation

```
  ╱────────────╲
 ╱   FOCUS      ╲
╱────────────────╲
│                 │
│ ● To study the  │
│   BBC           │
│   serialisation │
│   of Roll of    │
│   Thunder, Hear │
│   My Cry.       │
│                 │
```

Introduction
A serialisation of *Roll of Thunder, Hear My Cry* has been produced by the BBC. It will give you a different perspective of the story.

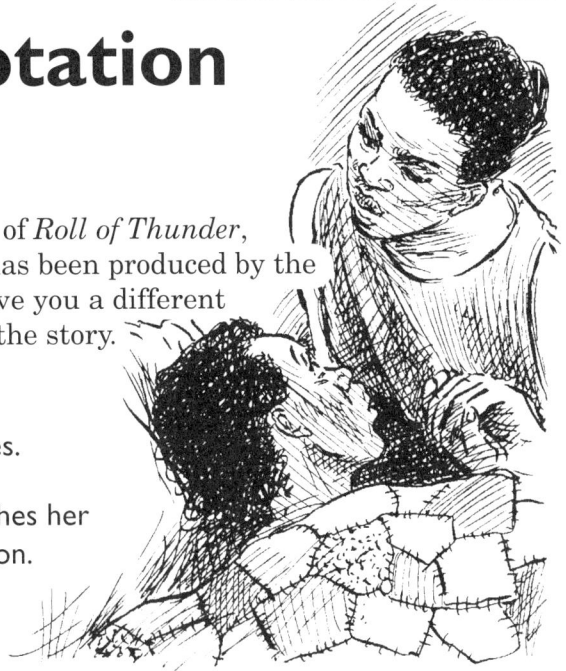

1. As you watch the video, focus on the following two scenes.

   - Mary Logan's discussion with Cassie in which she teaches her about black history and how to cope with discrimination. (Chapter 6)
   - The cotton fields on fire. (Chapter 12)

   As you watch, make notes under the following headings.

Is the scene as you imagined? If not, why?	What has been lost from the novel? Does this matter?	Do you gain anything by seeing the scene on video? If so, what and why?

2. After you have watched the video write a summary in answer to the following.
   Which scene is most suitable for adaptation and why? Refer to your notes.

3. Answer the following question in 300 words. What are the advantages and disadvantages of a television serialisation compared with a feature film of the novel?

Making comparisons

- To compare *Roll of Thunder, Hear My Cry* with *To Kill a Mockingbird*.

Introduction

Roll of Thunder, Hear My Cry is often compared with *To Kill a Mockingbird* by Harper Lee, which is also set in the Southern States in the 1930s. The narrator is a young white girl a few years younger than Cassie.

1. Read the passages below.

> First Purchase African M.E. Church was in the Quarters outside the southern town limits, across the old sawmill tracks. It was an ancient paint-peeled frame building, the only church in Maycomb with a steeple and bell, called First Purchase because it was paid for from the first earnings of freed slaves. Negroes worshipped in it on Sundays and white men gambled in it on weekdays.
>
> The churchyard was brick-hard clay, as was the cemetery beside it. If someone died during a dry spell, the body was covered with chunks of ice until rain softened the earth. A few graves in the cemetery were marked with crumbling tombstones; newer ones were outlined with brightly coloured glass and broken Coca-Cola bottles. Lightning rods guarding some graves denoted dead who rested uneasily; stumps of burned-out candles stood at the heads of infant graves. It was a happy cemetery.
>
> (Chapter 12, *To Kill a Mockingbird*)

> The Great Faith Elementary and Secondary School, one of the largest black schools in the county, was a dismal end to an hour's journey. Consisting of four weather-beaten wooden houses on stilts of brick, 320 students, seven teachers, a principal, a caretaker, and the caretaker's cow, which kept the wide crabgrass lawn sufficiently clipped in spring and summer, the school was located near three plantations, the largest and closest by far being the Granger plantation. Most of the students were from families that sharecropped on Granger land, and the others mainly from Montier and Harrison plantation families. Because the students were needed in the fields from early spring when the cotton was planted until after most of the cotton had been picked in the fall, the school adjusted its terms accordingly, beginning in October and dismissing in March.
>
> (Chapter 1, *Roll of Thunder, Hear My Cry*)

2. Discuss the following in pairs. Annotate the passage and make notes.
   a. In what important ways are the two passages similar? Consider the settings and subject matter and what kind of information you gain from the descriptions.
   b. What important differences do you notice? Think about the tone of the narrative voice. What mood does each voice suggest?

3. Now, write a summary of 150 words comparing the two passages. Refer to your notes.

Racism

FOCUS

- To identify and discuss different kinds of racism found in the novel.

Introduction

Racism is the dominant theme in the novel. It takes several forms and the victims deal with it in different ways.

- Work with a partner or in a group. Read the following quotations below and locate the incidents in the novel. Discuss the following points for each quotation and try to refer to other parts of the novel to support your ideas.

  - Is this an example of racism? If so, what kind? If not, try to explain what it means.

  - Explain how the victim deals with the incident and what the consequences are.

  Write up your answers for each example.

1. 'Holding the book up to her, I said, "See, Miz Crocker, see what it says. They give us these ole books when they didn't want 'em no more."' (Chapter 1)

2. '... "I know it and you know it, but he don't know it, and that's where the trouble is."' (Chapter 5)

3. 'R W stepped forward and slapped a reassuring hand on T J's shoulder. "That's right, T J. You name it and you've got it."' (Chapter 10)

4. '"Why don't you leave us alone? How come you always hanging 'round us anyway?"' (Chapter 3)

5. '"Not 'fore she 'pologizes to my gal, y'all ain't ..."' (Chapter 5)

MODERN CLASSICS: *Roll of Thunder, Hear My Cry*

Segregation

FOCUS

- To identify examples of segregation in the novel.

Introduction

Segregation is an aspect of racism and is constantly reinforced in the ways that the community is divided throughout the novel: by wealth and poverty (economic), by attending separate institutions (institutional), by not mixing together (social), and by having separate histories (historical).

1. Read the quotations below and decide what type of segregation each one depicts. (It may typify more than one, but choose the most important.) Copy and complete a table like the one below for your answers. Make notes explaining your choice in each case.

a. '... Little Man protested, "ifn that ole bus driver would slow down, I wouldn't get muddy!"' (Chapter 3)

b. '"... friendship between black and white don't mean that much 'cause it usually ain't on an equal basis."' (Chapter 7)

c. '"... there aren't enough of those same white people who ... would hang a white man for killing a black one."' (Chapter 7)

d. '"Mr Morrison lost his job ... and he ain't been able to find anything else."' (Chapter 2)

e. 'The Avery family share-cropped on Granger land.' (Chapter 1)

f. '"So now, even though seventy years have passed since slavery, most white people still think of us as they did then ..."' (Chapter 6)

g. '"Some folks tell me I can't remember what happened that Christmas – I warn't hardly six years old – but I remembers all right. I makes myself remember."' (Chapter 7)

Example	Economic	Institutional	Social	Historical
a.				

2. Make notes about two examples in the book where the black and white communities mix: one that is beneficial and one where the black community suffers. Select key quotations to support your choices.

MODERN CLASSICS: *Roll of Thunder, Hear My Cry*

Violence

FOCUS

- To identify an event and empathise with the victim of that event.

Introduction
Violence and the fear of violence is usually a consequence of racism in the novel. The children are constantly made aware of racism and deal with it in different ways.

1. Identify the following example of racism in the book and number the events in the correct sequence.

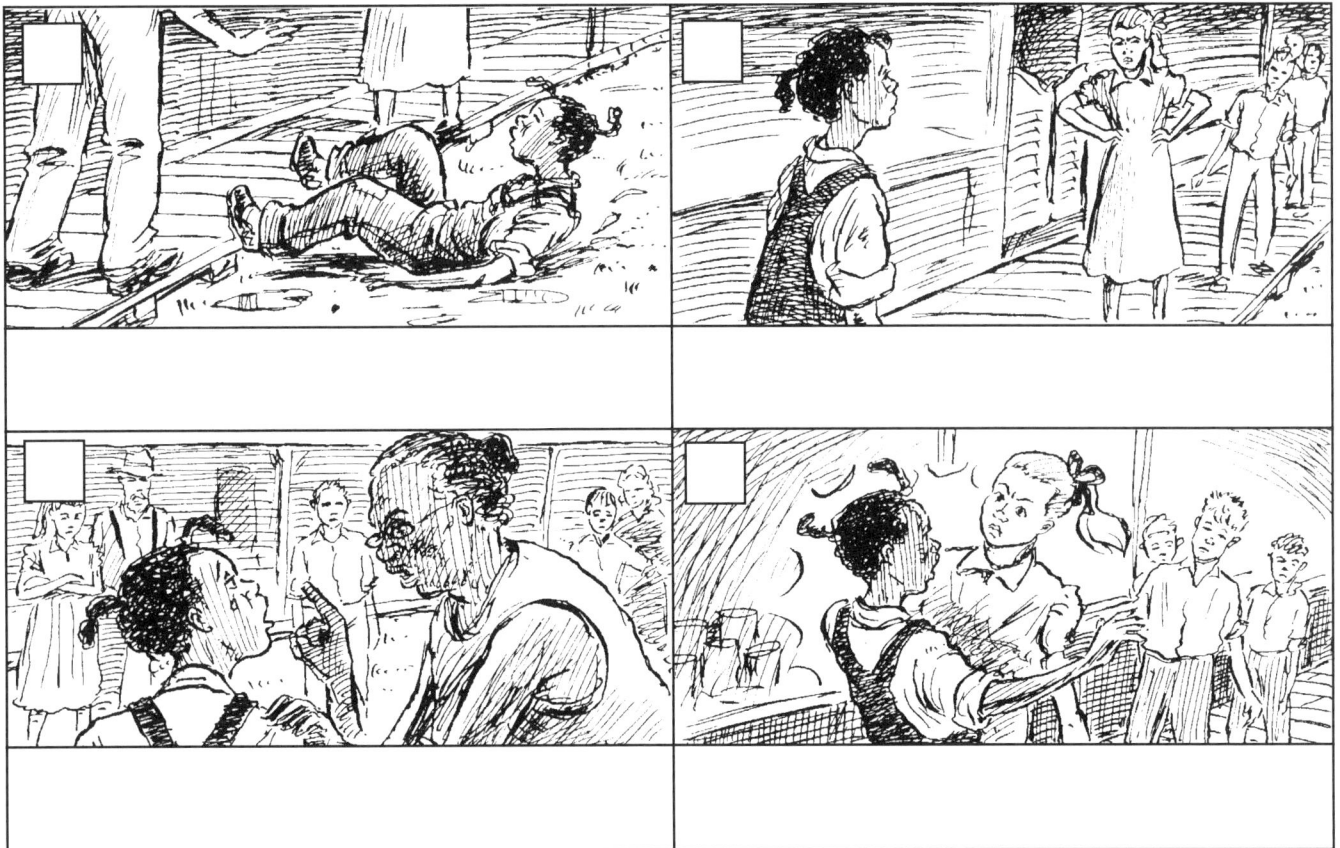

2. Write a caption under each picture to show what is happening.

3. Write down what revenge Cassie takes and what advice she is given by David Logan. (Compare this to the previous advice given by Mary Logan in Chapter 6.) Do you think Cassie is right to take the action she does? Give reasons for your answer.

4. How do you think Stacey would have dealt with this act of racism? In what way would it have differed from Cassie's reaction? Write your reply in 350 words. Refer to the book to support what you say.

Family life

FOCUS

- To identify examples of family life in the novel.

Introduction

Several examples of family life, including the ideal family, are presented in the *Roll of Thunder, Hear My Cry* and reveal the book's concern with the importance of the family as a role model for children.

1. Read the descriptions below and decide which family each refers to.

a. Though caring, the family struggles against insurmountable odds: poverty, illness and discrimination. Its inability to control a family member rebounds with tragic consequences.

b. They are a close-knit family who support each other. Conscious of their own history, they have a strong sense of justice and are respected in their community. The children learn important lessons about the harshness of the world but are also encouraged to practise tolerance.

c. A powerful, wealthy family rooted in the past, with a strong sense of identity and ownership, but with an inability to adapt to a changing world. The power it wields is usually to the disadvantage of others.

2. Now, find two other examples in the novel of family life and write a description of each one in the same style as above.

3. The Logan family has been described as the 'ideal family'. Write a paragraph saying whether or not you think this is true and, if so, why the author has chosen to present the Logans in this way.

The land

To understand the importance
of the land in the novel.

Introduction
The land is an important theme in the book and
symbolises several things. To the Logans it means
freedom, identity, and the future; to Harlan Granger it
means tradition, power and control.

1. Read the following quotations.

a.
'Mr Granger said quietly, "It was Granger land before
it was Logan."
"Slave land," said Papa.' (Chapter 7)

b.
'"You were born blessed, boy, with land of your own. If
you hadn't been, you'd cry out for it while you try to
survive ..."' (Chapter 9)

c.
'From deep in the field where the land sloped upward
toward the Granger forest, a fire billowed, carried
eastward by the wind.' (Chapter 12)

2. Now, read Pages 130–131, Chapter 7 when Big Ma asks Mr Jamison to secure the rights of the Logan land for her sons.

Use the information you have gathered to write an account about the land from Mr Jamison's point of view. Write in the first person and try to capture Mr Jamison's personality. (If you can, write in dialect, remembering that his will not be strong.) Include his attitude to Harlan Granger as well as his attitude to the Logans. You could begin:

I've lived in the South and the North but I'm a Southerner at heart. Couldn't live anywhere else, now. Don't get me wrong, though, there's plenty needs changing in the South. Take some folks, for instance ...

Quotations as evidence

FOCUS

- To provide advice on using quotations in essays.

Introduction
When you make an important statement about the novel you will need to support what you say by quoting from the text. Using quotations effectively will enhance your writing style as well as support your ideas and knowledge.

- There is some skill to using quotations. Sometimes you may wish to include the speaker and chapter. For example:

> The novel is set in the Southern States of America during the Depression of the 1930s. Cassie tells us in Chapter 1 that David Logan has to search for work, **'going as far north as Memphis and as far south as the Delta country.'**

- You can use ellipsis (...) to reduce the length of your quotation. For example:

> When Cassie sees Mr Berry's disfigurement, she witnesses the awful consequences of racism but also learns how to respect others, noting that **'Mama talked softly to both Mr and Mrs Berry ... as if Mr Berry were as normal as anyone else.'**

- You can also use more than one short quotation in a sentence.

> Mr Morrison, **'a human tree in height'** whose **'body bulged with muscles'** has agreed to protect the Logan family from racial harassment while Papa is away.

- Most importantly, however, you should try to incorporate your quotations in the sentence. Read through the examples again to check this.

- Refer to the chapters below. Combine the events and quotations into single sentences that make important points about the novel. Try to use quotations in different ways.

    1. Chapter 1. Cassie and the school text books. **'I could see that the covers of the books, a motley red, were badly worn and that the gray edges of the pages had been marred by pencils ...'**

    2. Chapter 3. Cassie observes Jeremy Simms. **'... I realised that Jeremy never rode the bus, no matter how bad the weather.'**

    3. Chapter 10. Uncle Hammer helps the family. **'"What good's a car? It can't grow cotton."'**

Stacey and Jeremy

FOCUS

- To write an essay in which you compare and contrast two characters.

Essay title

There are many ways in which Stacey Logan and Jeremy Simms are different but they also have some similarities. Compare and contrast their characters and say why their friendship is important in the book.

Planning

- **Stage 1:** First, think about suitable topics that relate to both characters and write them down. The list below has been done for you, but you may be able to add some more.

  - Their ages
  - What community they come from
  - Family life and relationships
  - Education
  - Attitude to others (including each other)
  - How they are treated by a variety of people
  - Their strengths and weaknesses

(Refer to any character sheets that might help you.)

- **Stage 2:** Now, make a column for each character and write notes in each column, referring to each topic heading (including those in the box above).

- **Stage 3:** Read through your notes and underline the differences between the two characters. Now underline in red any similarities between them. Consider their potential friendship.

- **Stage 4:** Add chapters, page references and a few quotations to support your main points.

- Now, write your essay.
  - Begin with Stacey.
  - Then, compare and contrast Jeremy with Stacey.
  - Conclude your essay by answering why their relationship is important in the book. To do this you will need to focus on the different communities they come from.

Family influences

FOCUS

- To write an essay in which you must consider who influences the main character.

Essay title

Cassie learns many things as she is growing up. Choose three family members and show how they influence her.

Planning

- **Stage 1:** Decide which family members to choose. Consider including a character who has a large influence (e.g. David Logan) and an unusual one to make your essay more interesting (e.g. Little Man). You could choose a third who is different from the other two, for instance, who has a different gender (e.g. Big Ma).

- **Stage 2:** Under the characters' names identify the most important way in which they influence Cassie and what evidence supports this. Add other points but do not list too many. You might begin like this:

David Logan
Teaches Cassie about her heritage (Page 12, Chapter 1)

Little Man
Encourages Cassie's feelings of loyalty during the 'school-book incident' (Page 27, Chapter 1)

- Now, begin your essay.

  - Start by saying that several family members influence Cassie in some way.
  - Then begin a new paragraph and show, in order, how each character influences her.
  - In your conclusion decide which character has the greatest influence and why. You will need to find evidence of this in the book.
    (Remember to consider the 'Author's Note' as well as the story.)

Black history

- To write an essay focusing on the historical circumstances behind the novel.

Essay title

What **evidence** is there that the **author** has an **understanding** of the **historical circumstances** behind the novel?

Planning

- **Stage 1:** This question is not as easy as it looks, because there are many historical factors that affect the novel. You therefore need to *mention* lesser points and *focus* on the most important ones. So, you need to have a good understanding of the background as well as the story. You could also choose different kinds of evidence, for example, reference to facts as well as reference to a character's viewpoints.

First identify the key words (key words identified in bold). You could ask yourself questions related to the key words and make notes. Copy and complete the following table.

Questions	Answers
What are the *most important* historical circumstances behind the novel?	Slavery, Civil War, Reconstruction, racism, Depression: the economic crisis and unemployment.
Evidence	(Page 11, Chapter 1) Cassie refers to Reconstruction, the financial crisis and unemployment during the 1930s. (Page 77, Chapter 4) Big Ma refers to the end of slavery and the freedom to purchase land and the economic consequences for the South after the Civil War.

You could also *mention* other factors, such as the death of David Logan's brother and Uncle Hammer's injury in the 1914–1918 War and the effect this has.

- **Stage 2:** Organise your notes and evidence so that you can write in coherent paragraphs.

- **Stage 3:** In conclusion, you could say that the *author's understanding* of the *historical circumstances* makes the reader aware that the Logan family view their history as separate from white history.

- Now, write your essay.

Exam passage

Read this passage carefully and then answer all questions that follow.

1　Little Man knew this too. His lips parted slightly as he took his hands from the book. He quivered, but he did not take his eyes from Miss Crocker. "I – I said may I have another book please, ma'am," he squeaked. "That one's dirty."

　"Dirty!" Miss Crocker echoed, appalled by such temerity. She stood up, gazing
5　down upon Little Man like a bony giant, but Little Man raised his head and continued to look into her eyes. "Dirty! And just who do you think you are, Clayton Chester? Here the county is giving us these wonderful books during these hard times and you're going to stand there and tell me that the book's too dirty? Now you take that book or get nothing at all!"

10　Little Man lowered his eyes and said nothing as he stared at the book. For several moments he stood there, his face barely visible above the desk, then he turned and looked at the few remaining books and, seeming to realize that they were as badly soiled as the one Miss Crocker had given him he looked across the room at me. I nodded and Little Man, glancing up again at Miss Crocker, slid the book from the
15　edge of the desk, and with his back straight and his head up returned to his seat.

　Miss Crocker sat down again. "Some people around here seem to be giving themselves airs. I'll tolerate no more of that," she scowled. "Sharon Lake, come get your book."

　I watched Little Man as he scooted into his seat beside two other little boys. He
20　sat for a while with a stony face looking out of the window; then, evidently accepting the fact that the book in front of him was the best that he could expect, he turned and opened it. But as he stared at the book's inside cover, his face clouded, changing from sulky acceptance to puzzlement. His brows furrowed. Then his eyes grew wide, and suddenly he sucked in his breath and sprang from his chair like a
25　wounded animal, flinging the book onto the floor and stomping madly upon it.

These questions are all based on the passage.

1. '"... during these hard times ..."' (Lines 7–8). Explain clearly what 'hard times' refers to.

2. Although defiant, Little Man is afraid of Miss Crocker. Find some words and phrases in the passage that indicate this.

3. Read lines 22–25 again. Why does Little Man's mood suddenly change? What does this tell you about him?

This question is based on the novel as a whole.

4. Write about an incident in which Miss Crocker, Mary Logan and Cassie feature. What does Cassie learn from the incident?

Exam questions

1. There are several examples of family life in the novel. Choose two families and show how they are different. Think about:

    —   what community they come from
    —   how they are regarded in the community
    —   what example they show their children
    —   how they support each other.

2. In what way is T J responsible for his own downfall? Think about his relationship with:

    —   R W and Melvin Simms
    —   his parents
    —   Mary Logan
    —   Stacey Logan.

3. Racial prejudice is an important part of the novel. Explain how it is shown. Think about:

    —   the night men
    —   the work on the plantations
    —   the Wallaces' shop
    —   Harlan Granger's attitude
    —   the school system.

4. The burning of the cotton fields is an important event in the novel. What does it tell you about:

    a. the land
    b. the black and white communities
    c. David Logan
    d. Wade Jamison?

5. There are several symbols in the book. Say what they are and explain what they mean. Think about:

    —   the weather
    —   the seasons
    —   the land
    —   other symbols of nature.

Further exam questions

1. It has been said that 'every story contains something useful'. What is the most useful thing you have learned from *Roll of Thunder, Hear My Cry* and why?

2. How do Cassie's weaknesses as well as her strengths help her to cope with the difficulties she encounters?

3. Explain what the important symbols in the novel represent and how they are closely related to each other.

4. Outline the similarities and differences between T J and Stacey and explain why one is a victim and the other a survivor.

5. 'I stared at her astonished. Then I turned and left the forest, not wanting to believe that Lillian Jean didn't even realise it had all been just a game.' Identify who is speaking and where in the novel, and explain what important point this incident makes about racism.

6. *Roll of Thunder, Hear My Cry* is an optimistic novel. Do you agree?

7. What are the most important things you learn about the Southern States of America in the 1930s through reading the novel? Explain in what ways the Northern States were different and why.

8. Choose two incidents from the novel and discuss the advantages of adapting one for the stage and the disadvantages of adapting the other.

9. Christopher-John is the odd one out amongst the Logans. Is this true?

Selected answers

Who says? (Page 18)

1. Mary Logan to Daisy Crocker about her stand on the condition of the school books and the unequal education offered to black pupils. (Page 31, Chapter 1)
2. Papa to Cassie about the importance of land. (Page 12, Chapter 1)
3. Mama to Cassie about the Lillian Jean incident and the need to make the right moral choices. (Page 107, Chapter 6)
4. Papa to the children about the likely outcome for T J. (Page 219, Chapter 12)
5. Mr Jamison to David Logan about the liberal view held by some white Southerners and about their lack of courage. (Pages 132–133, Chapter 7)
6. Uncle Hammer to David Logan about the danger the family faces from racism and the night men. (Page 190, Chapter 10)

The burning fields (Page 25)

1. a. Jeremy to Cassie and Christopher-John about how he thinks the fire started accidentally.
   b. Stacey to the Logan family about the fire diverting attention away from T J.
   c. Mr Jamison to David Logan, who started the fire as a decoy, about keeping a low profile and allowing the community to believe the fire started accidentally.

Speech and dialect (Page 26)

1. a. being difficult
   b. illegal selling of alcohol
   c. talking unwisely
   d. being miserable
   e. political adventurer from the Northern States
   f. a very long time, suggesting unhappiness
   g. has a legal right to particular land
   h. van or cart selling and delivering goods
2. Big Ma talking to Cassie (Page 77, Chapter 4)
4. Mary Logan talking to Cassie (Page 107, Chapter 6)

Similes and metaphors (Page 27)

Similes: 2, 3, 5 Metaphors: 1, 4, 6.

Symbols (Page 29)

1. a. The pearl-handled pistol can be seen to represent temptation, violence and ruin, associated with T J's downfall.
   b. The fig tree represents survival. (See David Logan's comment to Cassie, Page 166, Chapter 9.)

c. The night men represent extreme racism and violence as typified in the Ku Klux Klan and also in the behaviour of the Wallaces and the Simms.
   d. The thunder is the most important motif and represents danger from racial violence. It frequently occurs at such times in the novel. See also the novel's title and the blues song at the beginning of Chapter 11.
2. a. Autumn, the prospect of winter.
   b. Christmas and storytelling around the hearth.
   c. Spring, rain, life giving. Can be associated with Cassie's new-found lease of life at the end of the school year.
   d. The last day of the revival when there is summer heat and tension before the storm; a symbol of what is to come: the assault on T J, his arrest and the subsequent fire.
   e. The last page of the book depicts Cassie thinking about the remaining summer days when she and her brothers can run free, giving way to autumn rain and school. More importantly she associates these with the impact of recent events: T J's fate and the destruction of the land.

The narrative voice (Page 30)

1. The narrative voice in the first passage is of a young child puzzled by her father's words and struggling for meaning. Key words and phrases, such as 'looked at Papa strangely', 'one day I would understand. I wondered,' and use of pronouns such as, 'Mama', 'Papa', 'Uncle Hammer' suggest a child's voice.
2. In the second passage the more sophisticated language, pacing and grasp of the issues suggests an adult voice. The repetition of the verb 'learned' and the use of the term 'my father' reinforce this.

Racism (Page 35)

1. Institutionalised racism found in school.
2. Mr Barnett's blind, aggressive racism.
3. R W Simms' racist manipulation of T J.
4. Stacey's rejection of Jeremy.
5. Mr Simms' blind racism spilling into violence.

Segregation (Page 36)

1. a. institutional (education, the school bus)
   b. social
   c. institutional (the law)
   d. economic
   e. economic
   f. historical
   g. historical

Selected answers (continued)

Violence (Page 37)

1. The incident occurs when Cassie accidently bumps into Lillian Jean at Strawberry. (Chapter 5)

3	2
Mr Simms pushes Cassie into the dirt road.	Cassie apologises, but Lillian Jean refuses to let her past.

4	1
Big Ma tells Cassie to apologise to Lillian Jean.	Cassie accidentally bumps into Lillian Jean.

Family life (Page 38)

1. a. The Averys
   b. The Logans
   c. Harlan Granger's family.
2. Other examples might be: the Simms, the Wallaces and Mr Jamison and his wife.

Exam passage (Page 44)

1. The 'hard times' referred to by Miss Crocker are the Depression of the 1930s when resources for schools were limited. The Depression is referred to at other times in the book, for example, when in Chapter 1 Cassie refers to her father seeking work.
2. Phrases such as, 'He quivered', 'he squeaked', 'Little Man lowered his eyes', and 'he scooted into his seat'.
3. Little Man's mood suddenly changes (Lines 22–25) because he recognises something significant in the book's 'inside cover'. In the following passage we are told that this is a page recording who has used the book and how it has been treated. The clear discrimination between black and white students makes Little Man furious and further indicates that he will not suffer injustice easily.